THE SILVER COLLECTION
BOOK TWO

MORE ANTHEMS FOR
THE RSCM SILVER AND BISHOP'S AWARDS

RS✦M

COPYRIGHT INFORMATION AND ACKNOWLEDGMENTS

ISBN: 978-0-85402-238-0
RSCM Catalogue number: RAB80
Order number: B0393

Compiled by John Wardle
Edited by Tim Ruffer
Cover design by Smith & Gilmour
Music origination by David Iliff, MusicLines and the RSCM.
Printed in Great Britain

CONTENTS

No.	Composer	Title	Page
1	Anon.	Rejoice in the Lord alway	1
2	Anton Bruckner	Locus Iste	10
3	William Byrd	Ave verum corpus	15
4	Andrew Carter	For the beauty of the earth	23
5	Herbert Howells	Like as the hart desireth the waterbrooks	30
6	Henry Loosemore	O Lord, increase our faith	39
7	William Mathias	Lift up your heads, O ye gates	43
8	Felix Mendelssohn	How lovely are the messengers	50
9	Thomas Morley	Nolo mortem peccatoris	60
10	Max Reger	Unser lieben Frauen Traum	66
11	Richard Shephard	Song of Mary	70
12	Thomas Tallis	O Lord, give thy Holy Spirit	79
13	Tomás Luis de Victoria	Jesu, dulcis memoria	86
14	Samuel Sebastian Wesley	O Lord my God	89
15	Ian Wicks	We three kings	94

Training notes by John Wardle	104
RSCM Silver Award syllabus	111
RSCM Silver Award Marking Criteria	124

INDEX OF THEMES, FEASTS AND SEASONS

Title	Composer	No.	Page
Advent			
Rejoice in the Lord alway	Anon.	1	1
How lovely are the messengers	Mendelssohn	8	50
Epiphany			
We three kings	Wicks	15	94
Lent			
Like as the hart desireth the waterbrooks	Howells	5	30
O Lord, increase our faith	Loosemore	6	39
O Lord my God	S. S. Wesley	14	90
Mothering Sunday			
Song of Mary	Shephard	11	70
Passiontide & Holy Week			
Nolo mortem peccatoris	Morley	9	60
Unser lieben Frauen Traum	Reger	10	66
Eastertide			
Song of Mary	Shephard	11	70
Ascensiontide			
Lift up your heads, O ye gates	Mathias	7	43
Pentecost			
O Lord, give thy Holy Spirit	Tallis	12	79
Corpus Christi			
Ave verum corpus	Byrd	3	15
Harvest			
For the beauty of the earth	Carter	4	23

Title	Composer	No.	Page
Christus the King			
Lift up your heads, O ye gates	Mathias	7	43
Dedication festivals			
Locus iste	Bruckner	2	10
Holy Communion			
Ave verum corpus	Byrd	3	15
Jesu dulcis memoria	Victoria	13	86

PREFACE

The latest RSCM Silver Award syllabus revision offers a uniform, and increased, choice of Section A music to candidates in all of our Areas. This book contains 15 such anthems, written for SATB voices, in addition to the 30 already published in the RSCM *Silver Collection Book One*. They feature in List G, 51–65.

For singers in choirs of different forces, such as upper voices, there is now additional provision in Lists G and H.

I wish you every success at Silver level, and I hope you will look on preparing for your exam as a major stepping-stone in your *RSCM Voice for Life* training. We hope the scheme will help you along the road to vocal success, and continue a blessed ministry of music within your Christian community. Enjoy every anthem you sing!

JOHN WARDLE
Uppingham
Epiphany 2014

1. Rejoice in the Lord alway

Words: Philippians 4. 4–7

Music: ANON. (mid-16th century)
edited by Robert King

10

re - joice   in the Lord____ al - way,   and a-gain

say, re - joice,   re - joice   in the Lord   al - way,   and   a -

____ re-joice,   re - joice   in the Lord   al - way,____   and a-

say, re-joice,   re - joice   in the Lord   al - way,   and a-gain

15

I say,   re - joice,   re - joice   in the Lord_____ al-way,

-gain,   and   a - gain I say,   re - joice,   I say,____ re-joice,

-gain I say, re - joice,   re - joice__ in the Lord__ al-way,   in the Lord

I   say, re-joice,   re - joice   in the Lord   al - way, and a-gain I say, re-joice,   and a-gain

and a-gain I say, re-joice,   and a-

al - way,   and a - gain I say, re-joice, and a -

and a-gain I say, re-joice,   and a-gain I say, re - joice, a -

I say, re - - joice. Let your soft - ness be known un -

-gain I say, I say, re-joice. Let your soft - ness be known un -

-gain I say,_____ re - joice. Let your soft - ness be known un -

-gain I_____ say, re - joice. Let your soft - ness be known un -

29

-to all men,   let your soft - ness be known___ un - to all men:

-to all men,   let your soft - ness be known___ un - to all men:

-to all men,   let your soft - ness be known___ un - to all men: the

-to all men,   let your soft - ness be known___ un - to all men:

34

the   Lord___ is e'en at hand,   at   hand.

the   Lord   is   e'en at hand,   the   Lord___ is e'en at

Lord   is   e'en at hand, the   Lord   is   e'en   at   hand.

the   Lord___ is e'en at hand,   the   Lord   is   e'en at hand.

39
Be care - ful___ for no - thing: but in all pray-er and
hand. Be care - ful for no - thing: but in all pray-er and
Be care - ful for no - thing: but in all pray-er and
Be care - ful for no - thing: but in all pray-er and

45
sup-pli - ca - ti - on let your pe - ti - ti-
sup - pli-ca - ti - on let your pe - ti - ti-ons, let your pe - ti - ti -
sup-pli - ca - ti - on let your pe - ti - ti - ons, let your pe - ti - ti-ons be
sup-pli - ca - ti - on let your pe - ti - ti-ons, let your pe - ti - ti - ons

50
-ons be ma - ni - fest un - to
-ons be ma - ni-fest
ma - ni-fest un - to God, be ma - ni - fest, be ma - ni - fest un - to
be ma - ni - fest un - to God, be ma - ni - fest, be ma - ni-fest

55
God with giv - ing of thanks, with giv - ing of thanks.
un - to God with giv - ing of thanks, with giv - ing of thanks.
God with giv - ing of thanks, with giv - ing of thanks.
un - to God with giv - ing of thanks, with giv - ing of thanks.

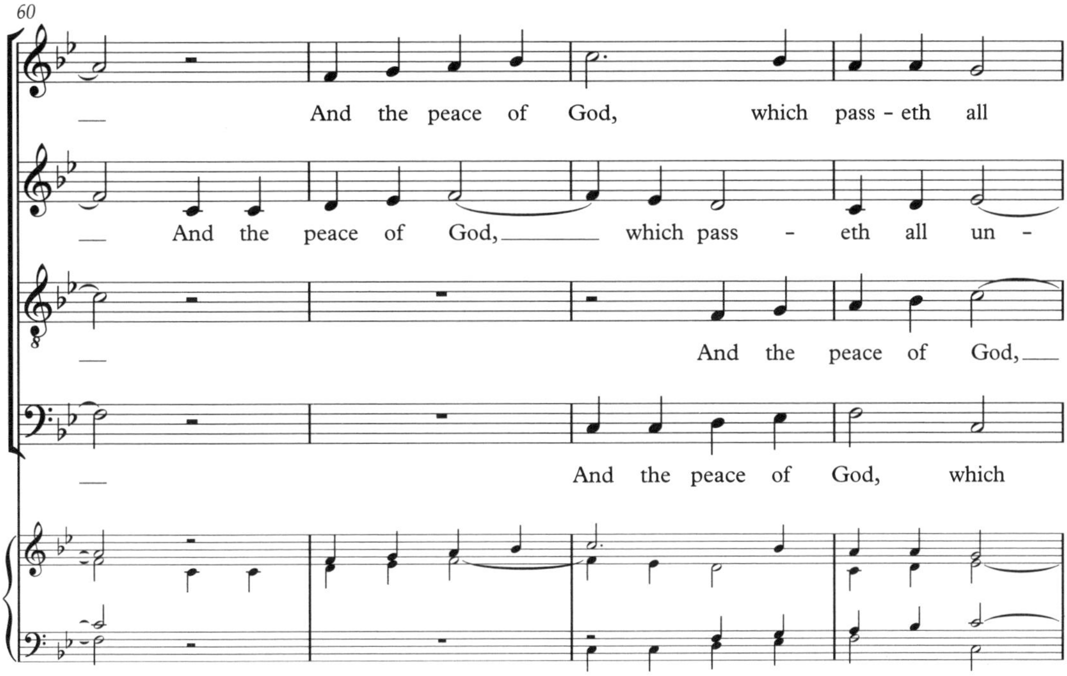
60
And the peace of God, which pass - eth all
And the peace of God, which pass - eth all un -
And the peace of God,
And the peace of God, which

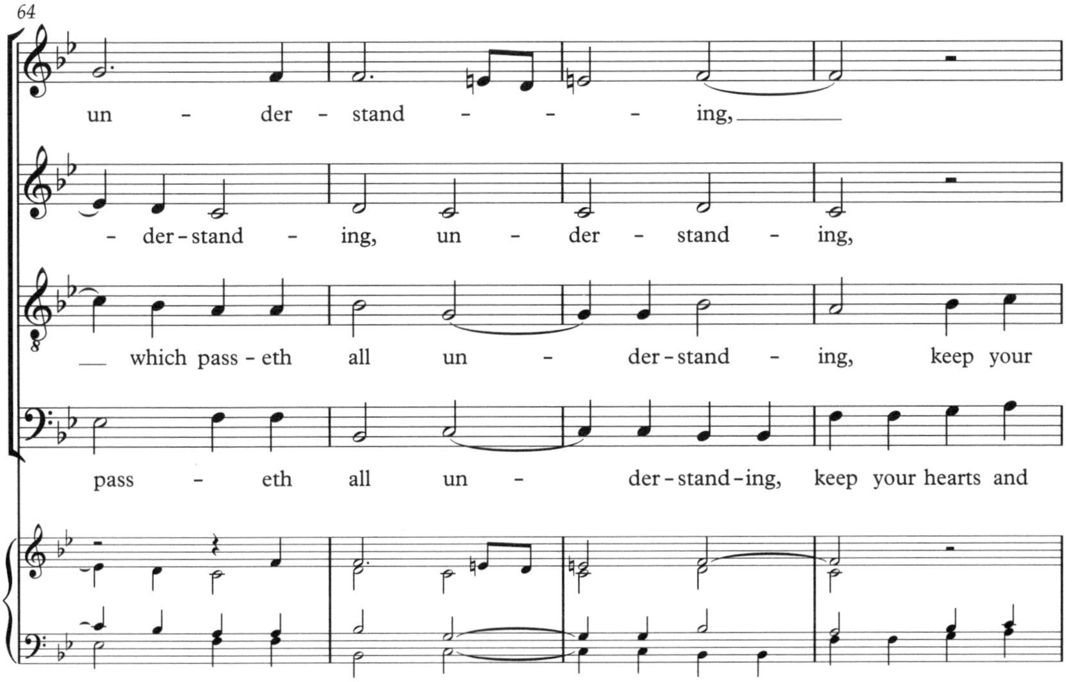
64
un - der - stand - - - ing,
- der - stand - ing, un - der - stand - ing,
which pass - eth all un - der - stand - ing, keep your
pass - eth all un - der - stand - ing, keep your hearts and

68

keep   your   hearts and   minds_____ through Christ

keep your   hearts   and minds through Christ   Je   -   -   -   su,

hearts and minds   through Christ Je   -   su, through   Christ   Je   -   su,

minds,   your   hearts   and minds through Christ Je   -   -   su,   keep your

72

Je - su,_____   keep your   hearts and   minds_____ through Christ

keep your   hearts   and minds   through Christ,   through

keep your   hearts and minds,   your hearts   and   minds   through Christ

hearts and   minds_____ through Christ   Je   -   -   su,   through Christ

76
Je - su, through Christ Je - su. A - - -
Christ Je - - su. A - - - -
Je - su, through Christ Je - su. A - -
Je - su, through Christ Je - su. A -

80
- men, a - - - - men.
- - men, a - - - - men, a - men.
- - - men, a - - - men, a - men.
- - - - - men, a - - men.

2. Locus iste

Words: Gradual for the Dedication of a Church

Music: ANTON BRUCKNER (1824–1896)
edited by David Hill

Allegro moderato

SOPRANO: Lo - cus i - ste   a De - o fa - ctus est,   lo - cus

ALTO: Lo - cus i - ste   a De - o fa - ctus est,   lo - cus

TENOR: Lo - cus i - ste   a De - o fa - ctus est,   lo - cus

BASS: Lo - cus i - ste a De - o fa - ctus est,   lo - cus

for rehearsal only

SOPRANO: i - ste   a De - o fa - ctus est,   a De - o,

ALTO: i - ste   a De - o fa - ctus est,   a De - o,

TENOR: i - ste   a De - o fa - ctus est,   a De - o,

BASS: i - ste a De - o fa - ctus est, a De - o,

De — o fa — ctus est in — ae — sti — ma — bi — le___

De — o fa — ctus est in — ae — sti — ma — bi — le___

De — o fa — ctus est in — ae — sti — ma — bi — le

De — o fa — ctus est in — ae — sti — ma — bi — le___ sa — cra —

sa — cra — men — tum, in — ae — sti — ma — bi — le___

sa — cra — men — tum, in — ae — sti — ma — bi — le___

sa — cra — men — tum, in — ae — sti — ma — bi — le

men — tum, in — ae — sti — ma — bi — le___ sa — cra —

19
pp
sa - cra - men-tum ir - re - pre-hen - si - bi-lis est,
pp
sa - cra - men-tum ir - re - pre-hen - si - bi-lis est,
pp
sa - cra - men-tum ir - re - pre-hen - si - bi-lis est, ir - re - pre-hen-
-men - tum
24
cresc.
p
mf
ir - re - pre -hen - si - bi-lis est, ir - re - pre - hen -
cresc.
p
mf
ir - re - pre -hen - si - bi-lis est, ir - re - pre - hen -
cresc.
mf
-si - bi-lis est, ir - re - pre - hen - si - bi-lis est, ir - re - pre - hen -

28
-si - bi-lis est._ Lo - cus i - ste a De - o fa - ctus est,
-si - bi - lis est._ Lo - cus i - ste a De - o fa - ctus est,
-si - bi-lis est. Lo - cus i - ste a De - o fa - ctus est,
Lo - cus i - ste a De - o fa - ctus est,
34
lo - cus i - ste a De - o fa - ctus est, a De - o,
lo - cus i - ste a De - o fa - ctus est, a De - o,
lo - cus i - ste a De - o fa - ctus est, a De - o,
lo - cus i - ste a De - o fa - ctus est, a De - o,

De - o, De – – – – – o,

De - o, De – – – – o,

De - o, De – – – – o,

De - o, De – – – – – o,

a De - o, De - o fa – – ctus est.

a De - o, De - o fa – – ctus est.

a De - o, De - o fa – ctus est.

a De - o, De - o fa – – ctus est.

3. Ave verum corpus

Words: Sequence in honour of the Blessed Sacrament,
14th century

Music: WILLIAM BYRD (c.1542–1623)
edited by Gordon Appleton

9

- re pas - sum,   im - mo - la - tum   in

- re pas - sum,   im - - mo - la - - tum

- re pas - sum,   im - mo - la - tum   in   cru -

- re pas - sum,   im - mo - la - tum   in

13

cru - ce_____ pro ho - mi - ne: Cu - jus la -

in   cru - ce pro ho - mi - ne: Cu - jus la -

- ce   pro   ho - mi - ne: Cu - jus la -

cru - ce_____ pro ho - mi - ne: Cu - jus la -

17
- tus per - fo - ra - - tum, un - da flu -
- tus per - fo - ra - tum, un - da flu -
- tus per - fo - ra - tum,
- tus per - fo - ra - tum, un -
20
- xit san - gui - ne, san - gui - ne. Es - to no -
- xit san - gui - ne, san - gui - ne. Es - to no -
un - da flu - xit san - gui - ne. Es - to no -
- da flu - - xit san - gui - ne. Es - to no -

-bis prae - gu - sta - tum in mor - tis___ ex - a -

-bis prae - gu - sta - tum in mor - tis, in mor - tis ex -

-bis prae - gu - sta - tum in mor - tis___ ex - a -

-bis prae - gu - sta - tum in mor - tis ex - a -

- mi - ne: O dul - cis! O pi - e! O

-a - mi - ne: O dul - cis, O pi - e,

- mi - ne: O dul - cis, O pi - e,___

- mi - ne: O dul - cis, O pi - e, O

32

Je - su___ fi - - li Ma - ri -

O Je - su fi - li Ma - ri -

___ O Je - su fi - li Ma - ri -

Je - su Fi - li Ma - ri -

35

- ae, mi - se - re - re me -

- ae, mi - se - re - re me - i, mi - se - re - re,

- ae, mi - se - re - re me - i, mi - se -

- ae, mi - se - re - re me - i,

39
-i, mi - se - re - re me - i, me -
mi - se - re - re me - i, mi - se - re - re me -
-re - re me - - i, me - i, mi - se -
mi - se - re - re me - i, mi - se - re - re me -

42
- - - i. O dul - cis! O pi -
- - - i. O dul - cis, O
-re - re me - i. O dul - cis, O
- - - i. O dul - cis, O

46
-e! O Je - su fi - - li Ma-ri -
pi - e, O Je - su fi - li Ma-ri -
pi - e, O Je - su fi - li Ma-ri -
pi - e, O Je - su Fi - li Ma - ri -

50
- ae, mi - se - re - re me -
- ae, mi - se-re - re me - i, mi - se-re - re,
- ae, mi - se-re - re me - i, mi - se-
- ae, mi - se-re - re me - i,

54
-i, mi - se - re - re me - i, me -
mi - se - re - re me - i, mi - se - re - re___ me -
-re - re me - - i, me - i, mi - se -
mi - se - re - re me - i, mi - se - re - re me -
57
- - i. A - - - men.
- - i. A - - - - - men.
-re - re__ me - i. A - - - - - men.
- - - i. A - - - - men.

4. For the beauty of the earth

Words: Folliott Sandford Pierpoint (altered)
(1837–1917)

Music: ANDREW CARTER (b.1939)

For the beauty of the earth is one movement from the longer work *Great is the Lord*
published by MorningStar Music Publishers of St Louis.

Fa-ther, un-to thee_ we raise_____ This our joy-ful hymn of praise.

Solo Flutes

2. For the

Solo off

(organ double
voices ad lib.)

beau - ty of each hour Of the day and of the night, Hill and vale, and tree and

30
mf cresc.
flower, Sun and moon and stars of light: Fa - ther, un - to thee we
mf cresc.
cresc,
35
f
raise This our joy-ful hymn of praise.
f
Solo Flutes
mf
mp
39
SOPRANO mf legato
For the
BASS and TENOR unis. mf legato
3. For the joy of ear and eye,
Solo off

heart   and brain's de-light,   For the   my - stic   har - mo-ny   Link-ing

sense   to sound and   sight:

Solo Flutes

cresc.

poco f

4. For the   joy   of hu-man   love,_____

poco f

Solo off

(organ double
voices ad lib.)

Bro-ther, sis-ter, pa-rent, child, Friends on earth and friends a-bove, For all

gen-tle thoughts and_ mild:_ Fa-ther un-to thee_ we raise_

This our joy-ful hymn of praise.

Solo

5. For each per - fect gift of thine To our race so free - ly giv'n, Gra - ces hu - man and di - vine, Flow'rs of earth and buds of heav'n:

Fa - ther un - to thee we raise

This our joy - ful hymn of praise!

5. Like as the hart desireth the waterbrooks

Words: Psalm 42.1–3

Music: HERBERT HOWELLS (1892–1983)

yea, e – ven for the_ liv – ing God._____

molto espressivo

dim. molto

When shall I come_____ to ap - pear_____ be-fore the

When_____ shall I come_____ to ap - pear_____

When shall I come_____ to ap - pear_____ be-fore the

When_____ shall I come_____ to ap - pear_____

molto espressivo

dim. molto

28
p
pre-sence of God?
be-fore God?
p
pre-sence of God?
p
be-fore God?
p
Più animato (un poco)
32
SOPRANO
mf
My tears have been my meat day and night,
Ch.
mp
Sw.
37
cresc.
molto
while they dai-ly say un - - to me,
3
cresc.
molto

Where,_____ where is now thy God?_____

My tears have been   my

TENOR and BASS UNISON

51
SOPRANO mf
My tears have been my meat
My
[mf]
meat day and night,
3

56
dim.
day and night, my meat day and night.
tears day and night, day and
mf My tears have been my meat day
dim.
mp
dim.
Man.

62
rall.
night.
and night.
p
mp
p
Ped.
Tempo primo, teneramente
67
p (Soprano in autograph ms.)
Like as the hart de - sir - eth the
p
Like as the hart de - sir - eth the wa - ter brooks,
TENOR and BASS
unison mp
Like as the hart de - sir - eth the wa - ter brooks, so long-eth my
Tempo primo, teneramente
pp

71

so long-eth my soul af - ter thee, O

soul af-ter thee, O God.

75

mp

God. My soul is a - thirst for

mf

My soul is a - thirst for God,

poco

poco

79

dim.

God, yea, for the liv - ing God.

yea, e - ven for the liv - ing God.

dim.

dolce ed ardente
rall.
mp
84
SOLO SOPRANO
(ad lib.)
When shall I come be -
mf
When shall I come to ap - pear
mf
When shall I come to ap -
mf
When shall I come to ap - pear
mf
When shall I come be -
dolce ed ardente
rall.
p

89
rit.
Lento assai
pp
- fore the pre - sence, the pre - sence of God?
be-fore the pre - sence, the pre - sence of God?
-pear be - fore the pre - sence of God?
be-fore the pre - sence, the pre - sence of God?
-fore the pre - sence, the pre - sence of God?
rit.
Lento assai
ppp
95
pp
ppp

6. O Lord, increase our faith

Music: HENRY LOOSEMORE (d. 1670)
edited by John Morehen

7
mp
en - due us with wis-dom, with wis - dom,
wis-dom, with wis - dom, en - due us with wis - dom, cha -
-due us with wis - dom, cha - ri - ty,
mp
en - due us with wis - dom, cha -
10
cha - ri - ty, chas - ti - ty, and pa - ti -
- ri - ty, chas - ti - ty, and pa - ti - ence, and pa - ti -
chas - ti - ty, and pa - ti - ence, and pa - - ti -
- ri - ty, chas - ti - ty, and pa - - ti -

13
-ence in all our ad-ver - si-
-ence in all our ad-ver - si -
-ence in all our ad-ver-si - ties, in all our ad-ver - si-
-ence in all our ad ver-si-ties, ad-ver - - - si -
16
p
mp
-ties. Sweet Je - sus, say A - - men, sweet
-ties. Sweet Je - sus, say A - men, sweet Je-sus, say A -
-ties. Sweet Je - sus, say A - men, sweet
-ties. Sweet Je - sus, say A - men, sweet

19
p
Je - sus, say A - men, sweet Je - sus, say A -
p
men, A - - men, sweet Je - sus, say A - men,
Je - sus, say A - men,
Je - sus, say A - - men,

22
- men, sweet Je - sus, say A - men.
sweet Je - sus, say A - men, say A - men.
p
sweet Je - sus, say A - men, say A - men.
p
sweet Je - sus, say A - men, say A - men.

7. Lift up your heads, O ye gates

Words: Psalm 24. 7–10

Music: WILLIAM MATHIAS (1934–1992)

and the King of glo - ry___ shall come in.___

Ped. (8'+16')

Who is this King of glo - ry? Who

Ped.

is this King of glo - ry? Who is this King of glo - ry?

The Lord strong___ and migh-ty, the Lord strong___ and migh-ty, the Lord migh-ty in bat-tle.

Lift up your heads, O ye gates,___   Lift up your heads, O ye

gates,___   e - ven lift them up,___ ye ev-er - last-ing doors,   and the

King of glo - ry____ shall come in.____

Who is this King of glo-ry?   Who is this King of glo-ry?

Who is this King of glo-ry? The Lord_____ of

Man.

hosts, the Lord_____ of hosts, the Lord_____ of

hosts,_ he___ is the King of glo - - ry,

glo - - ry, glo - - ry, glo - ry.

8. How lovely are the messengers

Words: from Romans 10. 15, 18   Music: FELIX MENDELSSOHN (1809–1847)

13
preach us the gos-pel of peace! How love -
preach us the gos-pel of peace, how love - ly are the mes - sen-gers that

17
SOPRANO
A
f
To all the
ALTO
f
- ly are they that preach us the gos-pel of peace! To all the
TENOR
f
To all the
BASS
f
preach us the gos-pel of peace, the gos - pel of peace! To all the
A
f

na - tions   is gone forth the sound of their words,   to all_____ the

na - tions   is gone forth the sound of their words,   the sound_____

na - tions   is gone forth the sound of their words,   to all_____ the

na - tions   is gone forth the sound of their words,   to   all_____ the

na - tions   is   gone forth the sounds of their   words,_____   is

_____   is   gone,_____   is   gone   forth   the

na - tions   is   gone forth the sound of their

na - tions   is   gone,_____   is   gone forth the sound of their

28
gone forth the sound of their words.
sound of their words.
f
words, their words. How love - ly are the mes - sen-gers that
f
words, the sound. How
32
f
How love - ly are the mes - sen - gers that
f
How love - ly are the mes - sen - gers that
preach us the gos - pel of peace, the mes - sen - gers that
love - ly are the mes - sen-gers, the mes - sen - gers that

35
dim.
p
preach us the gos-pel of peace, they that preach us the
preach us, that preach us the gos - pel of peace, that preach us the
preach us, that preach us the gos -pel, the gos - pel of peace, that preach us the
preach us, that preach us the gos-pel of peace, the
39
B
gos - pel of peace. To all the na - tions is
gos - pel of peace.
cresc.
gos - pel of peace. To all
gos - pel of peace.

43
gone forth the sound of their words,
To all the na - tions is
the na - tions,
cresc.
To all

47
f
to all the na - tions is
f
gone forth the sound of their words, to all the na - tions is
f
to all the na - tions is
the na - tions,
cresc.
f

51
gone forth the sound of their words, is gone forth the sound of their
gone forth the sound of their words, is gone forth the sound of their
gone forth the sound of their words, is gone forth the sound of their
f
is gone forth the sound of their words, is
54
words, to all the na - tions is
words, to all the na - tions is
words, to all the na - tions is
gone forth the sound of their words, to all the na - tions is
f

57

gone forth the sound of their words, through-out all the lands their glad

gone forth the sound of their words, through - out all the lands their glad

gone forth the sound of their words, through-out all the lands their glad

gone forth the sound of their words, through-out all the lands their glad

61

C

ti - - dings.

ti - - dings. How love - ly are the mes - sen-gers that

ti - - dings.____

ti - - dings.____

dim.

p

65
p
How love - ly they that
preach us the gos - pel of peace, how love - ly are the mes - sen -
how love - - ly they that
how love - - ly thay that

69
p
preach us the gos - pel of peace, they that
- gers that preach us the gos - pel of peace, that
preach, that preach us the gos - pel of peace, that
preach us the gos - pel of

72
preach us the gos - pel of peace.
preach us the gos - pel of peace.
preach us the gos - pel of peace.
p
peace, the gos - pel of peace.
75
sf
p

9. Nolo mortem peccatoris

Words: Poem attributed to
John Redford (d.1547)

Music: THOMAS MORLEY (c.1557/8–1602)
edited by Robert King

10
Fa - ther, I am thine on - ly Son,
Fa - ther, I am thine on - ly Son, Sent down from heav'n, man -
Fa - ther, I am thine on - ly Son, Sent down from heav'n, man - kind to
Fa - ther, I am thine on - ly Son,
mf
14
Sent down from heav'n, man - kind to save. Fa - ther, all
kind to save, sent down from heav'n, man - kind to save. Fa -
save, man - kind to save, sent down from heav'n, man - kind to save. Fa -
Sent down from heav'n, man - kind to save, man - kind to save. Fa -

18
things ful - fill'd and done Ac - cord - ing to thy will, thy will, I
ther, all things ful - fill'd and done Ac - cord - ing to thy will, I
ther, all things ful - fill'd and done Ac - cord - ing to thy will, I
ther, all things ful - fill'd and done Ac - cord - ing to thy will, I
22
have. Fa - ther, my will now all is this: No - lo mor - tem pec -
have. Fa - ther, my will now all is this: No - lo mor -
have. Fa - ther, my will now all is this: No - lo mor -
have. Fa - ther, my will now all is this: No - lo mor -
mp

26
-ca - to - - ris. Fa - ther, be - hold my pain - ful smart,
-tem pec - ca - to - ris. Fa - ther, be - hold my pain - ful smart,
-tem pec - ca - to - ris. Fa - ther, be - hold my
-tem pec - ca - to - ris. Fa - ther, be -
mf
31
Ta - ken for man on ev - 'ry side. Ev'n
Ta - ken for man on ev - 'ry side, on ev - 'ry side. Ev'n
pain - ful smart, Ta - ken for man on ev - 'ry side.
-hold my pain - ful smart, Ta - ken for man on ev - 'ry side.

35
from my birth to death most tart No kind of pain I have de-
from my birth to death most tart, to death most tart No kind of pain I
Ev'n from my birth to death most tart No kind of pain I
Ev'n from my birth to death most tart No kind of pain I

40
- nied, But suf-fered all, and all for this: No - lo mor-tem pec-
have de - nied, But suf-fered all, and all for this: No - lo mor - tem pec-
have de - nied, But suf-fered all, and all for this:
have de - nied, But suf-fered all, and all for this:

45
- ca - to - ris, no - lo mor - tem
- ca - to - ris, no - lo mor -
No - lo mor - tem pec - ca - to - ris,
No - lo mor-tem pec - ca - to - ris, no-
dim.

50
pec - ca - to - ris, no - lo mor - tem pec - ca - to - ris.
-tem pec - ca - to - ris, no - lo mor-tem pec - ca - to - ris.
no - lo mor-tem pec - ca - to - ris, pec - ca - to - ris.
- lo mor - tem pec - ca - to - ris, pec-ca - to - ris.
p

10. Unser lieben Frauen Traum
Our Lady's Dream

Words: German traditional
English version: Catherine Winkworth

Music: MAX REGER (1873–1916)
Op.138 No.4

Zart bewegt [Con molto dolce] (♩ = 104)

SOPRANO
ALTO

1. Und un - ser lie - ben Frau - en Der trau - met, trau - met
1. Our La - dy lay a - sleep - ing And dreamed a dream, as

TENOR
BASS

ihr____ ein Traum: Wie un - ter ih - rem Her - zen Ge -
e'er____ 'tis said: That there___ be - neath her heart____ lay A

-wach - sen wär, ge - wach - sen ein Baum. 2. Und wie___ der Baum ein Schat - ten
tree___ that grew with bran - ches out-spread. 2. And lo,___ the tree___ its sha - dow

20

gäb Wohl ü – ber al – le, al – le Land: Herr Je – sus
gave To shel – ter ev – 'ry, ev – 'ry land: Lord Je – sus

26

Christ der Hei – land Al – so ist er, ist er ge – nannt.
Christ our Sa – viour, That tree is he, and aye shall stand.

33

Herr Je – sus Christ der Hei – land ist un – ser Heil und
Lord Je – sus Christ, our sa – ving health, hears us when we

Herr Je – sus Christ der Hei – land ist un – ser Heil und
Lord Je – sus Christ, our sa – ving health, hears us when we

Herr Je – sus Christ der Hei – land ist un – ser Heil und
Lord Je – sus Christ, our sa – ving health, hears us when we

Herr Je – sus Christ der Hei – land ist un – ser Heil und
Lord Je – sus Christ, our sa – ving health, hears us when we

Trost: Mit sei - ner bit - tern___ Mar - ter hat er uns
call: By his most bit - ter___ Pas - sion He hath re -

Trost: Mit sei - ner bit - tern___ Mar - ter hat er uns
call: By his most bit - ter___ Pas - sion He hath re -

Trost: Mit sei - ner bit - tern Mar - ter hat er uns
call: By his most bit - ter Pas - sion He hath re -

Trost: Mit sei - ner bit - tern Mar - ter hat er uns
call: By his most bit - ter Pas - sion He hath re -

ritardando
43
S.1
uns all er - lost.
re - deemed us all.
all er - lost, hat er uns all er - lost.
-deemed us all, He hath re - deemed us all.
all er - lost, hat er uns all er - lost.
-deemed us all, He hath re - deemed us all.
all er - lost, hat er uns all er - lost.
-deemed us all, He hath re - deemed us all.
all er - lost, hat er uns all er - lost.
-deemed us all, He hath re - deemed us all.
ritardando

11. Song of Mary
My Lord and Saviour is my song

Words: Mary Holtby
after Luke 1.46–55

Music: RICHARD SHEPHARD (b. 1949)

Con moto ♩ = 120

ORGAN

Ped.

My Lord and Sa - viour is my

UNISON *f*

song, He fills my spi - rit with de - light____ To

13
raise me up his arm is strong, The low - ly pre - cious
17
in his sight.
(unison ad lib.) ff
Mag - ni - fi - cat,
ff
(organ ad lib.)
21
Mag - ni - fi-cat
Mag - ni - fi-cat,
Mag - ni - fi-cat
Mag - ni - fi-cat

25

a - ni-ma me - a Do – mi – num.

f

dim.

(Man.)

29

SOPRANO and ALTO UNISON

mp

My name shall live from age to age,   And ev - 'ry tongue his

mp

33

cresc.

ser - vant bless,_____ For mer-cy is their he - ri-tage_____

37

___ Whose hearts_____ the Ho - ly One con-fess.

41
f
Mag - ni - fi - cat,
Mag - ni - fi-cat,
f
(organ ad lib.)
f
45
Mag - ni - fi-cat
Mag - ni - fi - cat
a - ni-ma me - a Do - mi-num.
Mag - ni - fi-cat
Mag - ni - fi - cat
Man.
49
TENOR and BASS UNISON
f
The proud be - guil'd by dreams of
8'+16'
Ped.

pow'r   Di – vi-ded and de - gra - ded lie:_____   He casts them down from

throne and tow'r____ And stoops____ to lift the hum – ble high.

Man.

SOPRANO (and ALTO) UNISON

Mag - ni - fi-cat,   Mag - ni - fi-cat,   Mag

TENOR and BASS UNISON

Mag - ni - fi cat,   Mag - ni - fi-cat, Mag

Sw. *mp*   Gt. *f*   Sw. *mp*   Gt. *f*   *ff*

68
p
-ni - fi-cat a - ni-ma me - a Do - mi-num.
p
p
72
p
He feeds the hun-gry at his board And sends the rich un-
p
(organ double voices ad lib.)
77 -fill'd a - way, And mind-ful of his pro - mis'd word
-fill'd a - way, And mind - ful of his pro-mis'd word

Has an - swer'd

Has an - swer'd Is - rael's prayer to - day.
Has an - swer'd Is - rael's prayer to - day.

f

Ped. ad lib.

f

Mag - ni - fi - cat,   Mag - ni - fi - cat,

f

Mag - ni - fi - cat

Mag - ni - fi - cat   a - ni-ma me - a   Do - mi-num.
Mag - ni - fi-cat

Mag - ni - fi - cat

(Man.)

With all the el - ders of our
race, And those un-born who seek this birth,_____ I sing the glo - ry
of his grace_____ Who brings_____ e - ter - ni - ty to earth.

106

Mag - ni - fi-cat,   Mag - ni - fi - cat,

111   **molto rit.**

SOPRANO
Mag - ni - fi-cat a - ni-ma me - a Do - mi-num.

ALTO
Mag - ni - fi-cat a - ni-ma me - a Do - mi - num.

TENOR
Mag - ni - fi-cat a - ni-ma me - a Do - mi - num.

BASS
Mag - ni - fi-cat a - ni-ma me - a Do - mi - num.

molto rit.

12. O Lord, give thy Holy Spirit

Music: THOMAS TALLIS (c. 1505–1585)

7
- stand - ing, that we may dwell in the fear of thy
- stand - ing, that we may dwell in the fear of thy
un - der - stand - ing, that we may dwell in the
un - der - stand - ing, that we may
10
Name, in the fear of thy
Name, in the fear of thy Name, in the fear of thy
fear of thy Name, in the fear of thy
dwell in the fear of thy Name, in the fear of thy

13
Name, all___ the days of our life,
Name, all___ the days of our life, all___ the days
Name, in the fear of thy Name, all___ the days
Name, in the fear of thy Name, all___ the days of our

16
all the days of our life, that we may
of our life, all the days of___ our___ life, that
of our life, all the days of___ our___ life, that
life, all the days of our life, that

19

know thee, the on - ly true God, and

we may know thee, the on - ly true God,

we may know thee, the on - ly true

we may know thee, the on - ly true God,

22

Je - sus Christ whom thou hast sent, and Je - sus

and Je - sus Christ whom thou hast sent, and Je -

God, and Je - sus Christ whom thou hast sent,

and Je - sus Christ whom thou hast sent, and

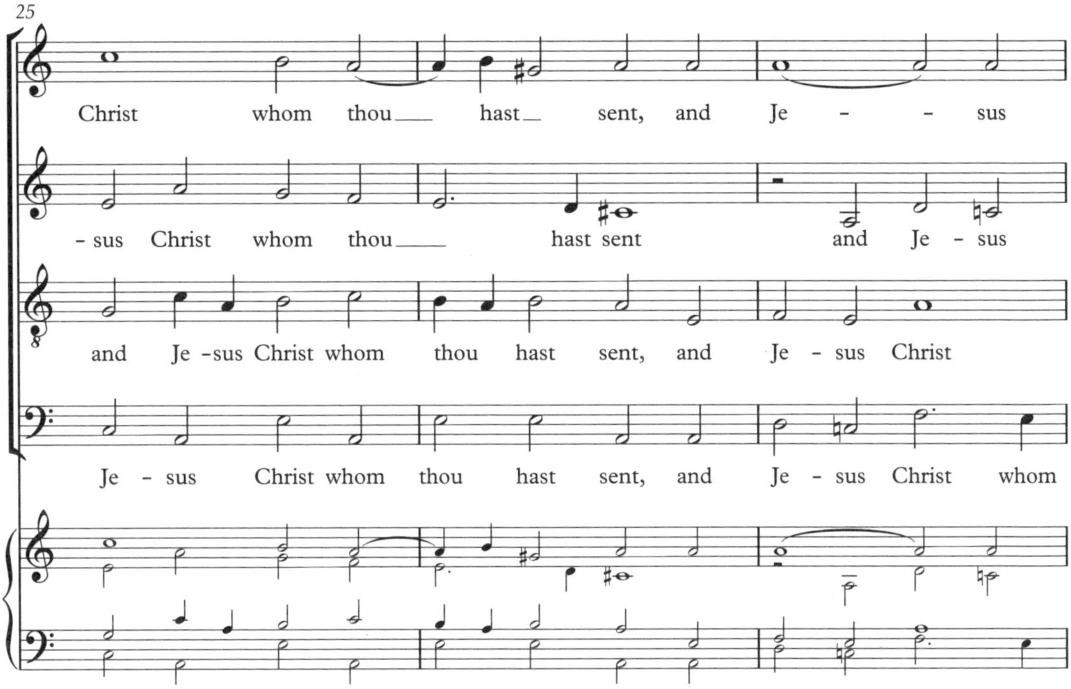
25
Christ whom thou hast sent, and Je - - sus
- sus Christ whom thou hast sent and Je - sus
and Je -sus Christ whom thou hast sent, and Je - sus Christ
Je - sus Christ whom thou hast sent, and Je - sus Christ whom

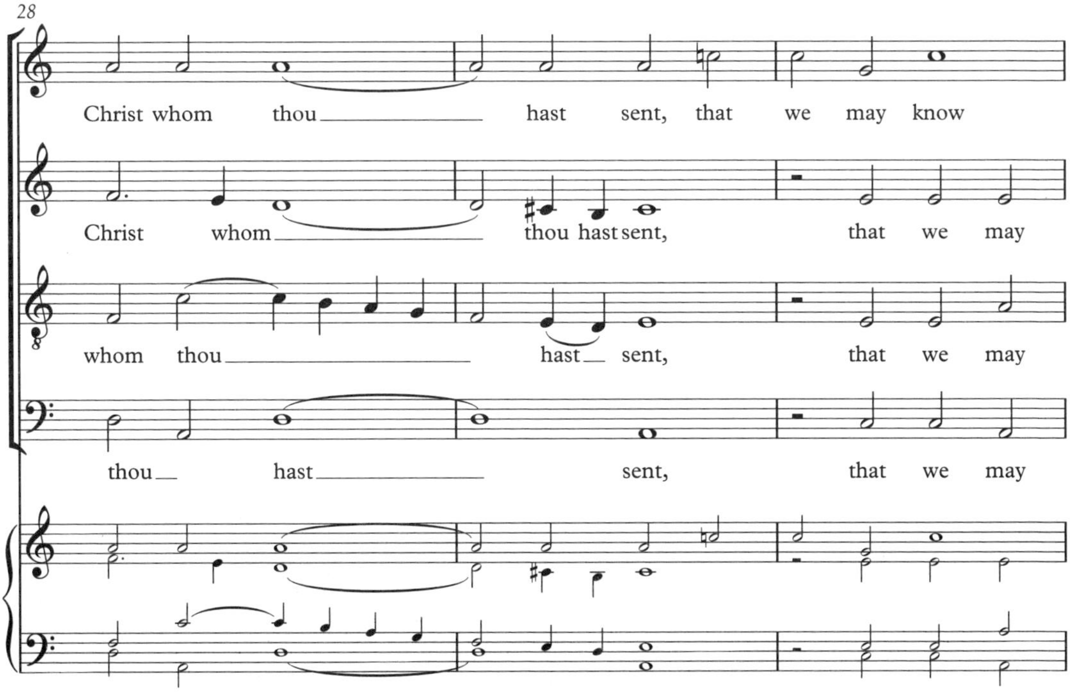
28
Christ whom thou hast sent, that we may know
Christ whom thou hast sent, that we may
whom thou hast sent, that we may
thou hast sent, that we may

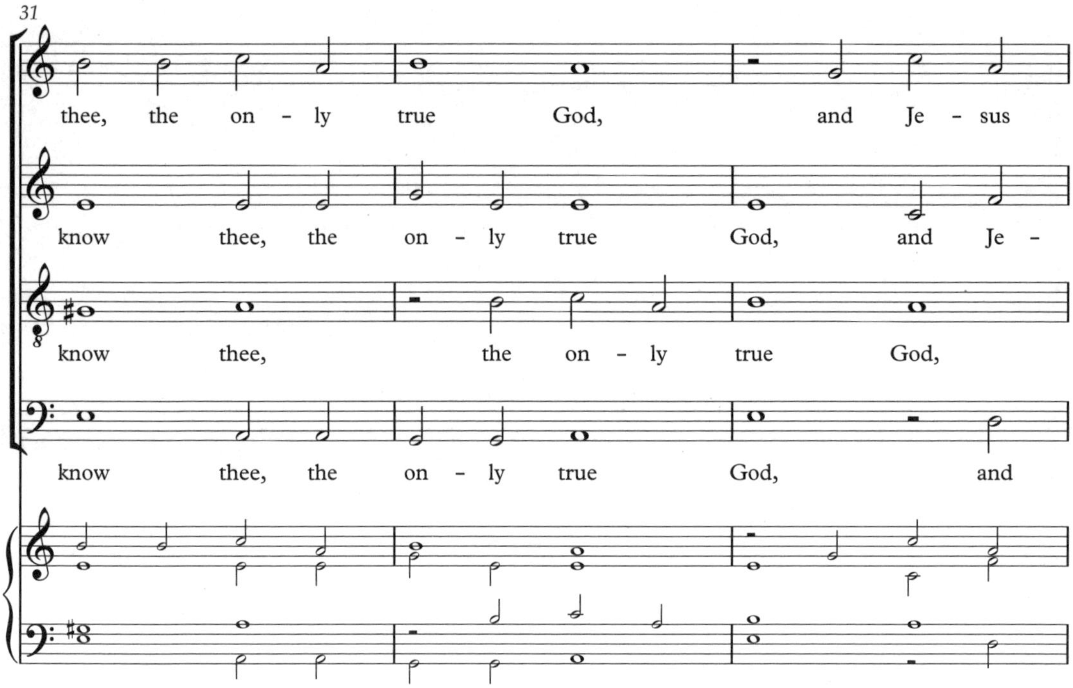
31
thee, the on - ly true God, and Je - sus
know thee, the on - ly true God, and Je -
know thee, the on - ly true God,
know thee, the on - ly true God, and

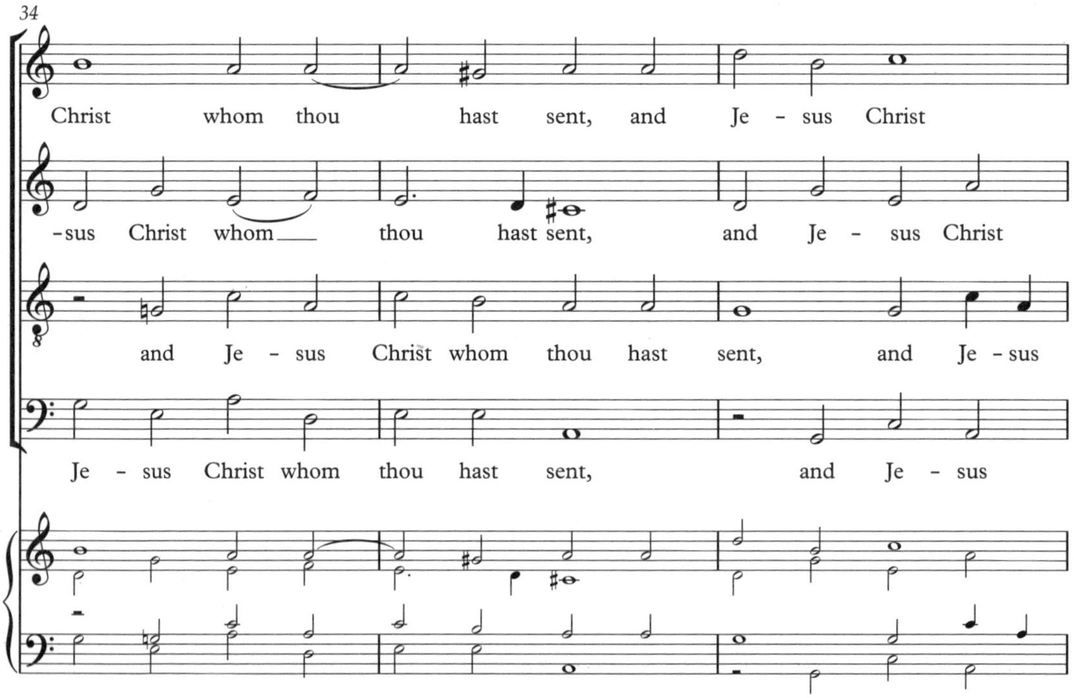
34
Christ whom thou hast sent, and Je - sus Christ
-sus Christ whom thou hast sent, and Je - sus Christ
and Je - sus Christ whom thou hast sent, and Je - sus
Je - sus Christ whom thou hast sent, and Je - sus

37
whom thou hast sent, and Je - - sus Christ whom
whom thou hast sent, and Je - sus Christ whom
Christ whom thou hast sent, and Je - sus Christ whom thou
Christ whom thou hast sent, and Je - sus Christ whom thou
40
thou hast sent.
thou hast sent.
hast sent.
hast sent.

13. Jesu, dulcis memoria

Words: attrib. Saint Bernard of Clairvaux

Music: *attributed to*
TOMÁS LUIS DE VICTORIA (1548–1611)
edited by Patrick Russill

Editorial note: original pitch retained, original note-values halved

10
ve - ra cor - di gau - di - a: Sed su-per mel et
gau - - - di - a: Sed su - -per mel et
ve-ra cor - di gau - di - a: Sed su - per mel
-di gau - di - a: Sed su-per mel et o -
14
o - - - - mni - a, su - per mel
o - - - - mni - a, su - - per mel et
et o - - mni - a, su - - - - per
mni - - - a, et

17
et o - mni - a, E - jus dul - cis prae - sen - ti - a, prae -
o - mni - a, E - jus dul - cis prae -
mel et o - mni - a, E - jus dul - cis prae - sen - ti -
o - mni - a, E - jus dul -
21
-sen - - ti - a.
sen - - ti - a, dul - cis prae - sen - ti - a.
-a, prae - sen - ti - a, dul - cis prae - sen - ti - a.
cis prae - sen - ti - a.

14. O Lord my God

Words: King Solomon's Prayer
Words suggested by I Kings. 8

Music: SAMUEL SEBASTIAN WESLEY (1810–1876)
edited by H. Watkins Shaw (1911–1996)

12
dim.
p
pray'r, re - spect un - to his prayer. Hear thou in
pray'r, re - spect un - to his prayer. Hear thou in
pray'r, re - spect un - to his prayer. Hear thou in
-spect, re - spect un - to his prayer. Hear thou in
18
heav'n thy dwell - ing place, And when thou hear - est,
heav'n thy dwell - ing place, And when thou hear - est,
heav'n thy dwell - ing place, And when thou hear - est,
heav'n thy dwell - ing place, And when thou

Lord,__ for - give,__ Hear thou in heav'n thy dwell - ing place,__

Lord,__ for - give, Hear thou in heav'n thy dwell - ing place,

Lord, for - give, Hear thou in heav'n thy dwell - ing place,__

hear - est, for - give, Hear thou in heav'n thy dwell - ing place,

And when thou hear - est, Lord, for - give,__ And when thou hear - est,

And when thou hear - est, Lord, for - give, And when thou hear - est,

And when thou hear - est, Lord, for - give, And when thou hear - est,

And when thou hear - est, Lord, for - give, And when thou hear - est,

35
p
Lord, for - give, for - give, for - give,
Lord, for - give, for - give, for - give,
Lord, for - give, for - give, for - give,
Lord, for - give, for - give, for - give,
41
mf
And when thou hear - est, Lord, for - give, for - give,
And when thou hear - est, Lord, for - give, for - give,
And when thou hear - est, Lord, for - give, for - give,
O Lord, for - give, for - give,

46
Either A
p
for - give,
And when thou hear - est, Lord, for -
And when thou hear - est, Lord, for -
give.
52
or B
cresc.
dim.
And when thou hear - est, Lord, for - give.

for Salisbury Cathedral School

15. We three kings

Words: John Henry Hopkins Jr.
(1820–1891)

Music: IAN WICKS
(b.1963)

13
star of won - der star of night, star with roy - al
16
beau - ty bright, west - ward lead - ing, still pro - ceed - ing
19
guide us to thy per - fect light.
21

ALL VOICES *ad lib.*

Born a king on Beth-le-hem plain, Gold I bring to crown him a-gain King for-e - ver, ceas-ing ne - ver o-ver us all to reign. O star of won - der star of night, star with roy - al beau - ty bright, west - ward lead - ing, still pro - ceed - ing, guide us to thy per - fect light.

Frank - in - cense to

of - fer have I; In - cense owns a Dei - ty nigh:

Prayer and prais - ing, all men rais - ing Wor-ship him God most high. O

star of won - der, star of night, star with roy - al beau - ty bright,

west-ward lead - ing, still pro-ceed-ing guide us to thy per - fect light.

59
a little slower with expression
mp
Myrrh is mine; its
mp
62
bit - ter per - fume breathes a life of ga - ther - ing gloom:
65
rit
p
sor-row-ing, sigh-ing, bleed-ing, dy - ing, sealed in the stone-cold tomb. O
p
69
poco a poco a tempo 1
mp
star of won - der, star of night, star with roy - al beau - ty bright,
mp

west-ward lead-ing,   still pro-ceed-ing,   guide us to   thy   per-fect light.

Glor - ious   now   be - hold him a - rise,   King   and   God   and

sa - cri-fice.   Heav'n sings Hal - le - lu - ia; Hal - le -

SOPRANO DESCANT
87
ff
O star of won - der, star of night,
ff
- lu - ia the earth re - plies. O star of won - der, star of night,
ff
ff

91
star with roy - al beau - ty bright, west - ward lead - ing,
star with roy - al beau - ty bright, west - ward lead - ing

still pro - ceed - ing   guide   us   to   thy   per - fect

still pro - ceed - ing   guide   us   to   thy   per - fect

light.

light.

light.

TRAINING NOTES
WITH GUIDE TO VOCAL RANGES

1. Anon.: Rejoice in the Lord alway   *Page 1*

- St Paul's Letter to the Philippians, in which he refers to his imprisonment in Rome and impending trial, is suffused with Christian optimism: no more so than in this famous exhortation to rejoice.

- The anonymous composer has captured something of the uplifting mood, with a characteristic opening motif of rising intervals that perfectly match the inflection of the text. You will sing this motet with measured tonal warmth and exhilaration.

- Set a tempo that reflects the minim pulse, and is energetic, but in a controlled style without any loss of precision.

- Although no dynamics are indicated, be alert to their varied use. No phrase should be unremittingly *f*, rather the few climaxes (*and again…, for nothing, with giving of thanks, hearts and minds…*) should be expectantly awaited. In other places, there is opportunity for a warm and effective *mp* to be used.

- It may be best to avoid any alteration of tempo as you sing *And the peace of God…* but this point, perhaps the quietest of all, certainly needs mellifluous tone and delicate phrasing. If you maintain the opening tempo here, you will then have the opportunity to relax it subtly at bar 77, leading into an expressively controlled ending.

- In the final 5 bars, every voice has considerable underlay in the repeated *Amens*, so you should only breathe at given commas.

2. Bruckner: Locus iste   *Page 10*

Translation: This place was made by God, a priceless sacrament; it is without reproach.

- A setting of traditional words for the dedication of a Church. The piece touches on our awareness of a building, but it also conveys something of the sense of the presence of God.

- A very precise, quiet, start is essential. The soprano line needs exquisite tuning throughout, but particularly the second note, the leading-note, must be brightly centred.

- The pace must be reliably maintained throughout with precise counting. Even the moment of silence, 2 beats before the reprise, can be magically reflective, within this same precise context. Do not be tempted to romanticise your performance with any rubato.

- The dignified, glowing sounds this piece demands will be achieved with the use of resonant, controlled tone and great care in placing the singer's breaths.

- Dynamic interest, within a wide but tonally controlled spectrum, can create a magical effect. Every detail in the score will enhance this, particularly if the *ff* climax is reached strongly, majestically and with no hint of forced tone.

3. Byrd: *Ave verum corpus* Page 15

Translation: Hail, true Body, born of the Virgin Mary, who having truly suffered, was sacrificed on the cross for mankind, whose pierced side flowed with water and blood: May it be for us a foretaste [of the Heavenly banquet] in the trial of death.

O sweet Jesus, O pious Jesus, O Jesus, son of Mary, have mercy on me. Amen.

- This wonderfully restrained motet is another gem of vocal writing from the Tudor period. Aim to maintain a pace that is very reliable, whilst allowing the singer to shape each phrase with excellent control. You might experiment in rehearsal to achieve the tempo that best succeeds, not only technically, but also expressively.

- Although no dynamics are indicated, your understanding of the text (and appreciation of Byrd's tonal framework) will give you a very clear idea of the overall contours of the piece, which will be quietly vibrant, not static. The warm intensity of *O dulcis, O pie, O Jesu…* will ideally captivate the listener. Develop all such climaxes very alertly, finishing with a quiet and meaningful *Amen*.

- It is very important that the text is clearly focused, and all the Latin vowels must be precise and un-anglicised, pure in quality. This success will help the precision of your tuning, too.

- William Byrd remained a faithful Catholic, despite living through a period of religious turmoil. His treatment of the words therefore fully reflects his understanding of their meaning. So should our performances, in this day and age. It is a piece really to explore and enjoy!

4. Carter: *For the beauty of the earth* Page 23

- This lively and engaging anthem has a dance-like quality which you should cultivate in your singing. By phrasing it sensitively, the meaning of the text will gain immediacy for the listener.

- You might take the opportunity to 'sing through' longer phrases (such as bars 11-14), and to 'feel' rather than to articulate the commas in bar 54; but the shaping of the refrain poses a dilemma – might it be thought of as one, two or even three phrases? And must that be consistent? Clearly, the final refrain cannot be, which might offer you a glimpse of freedom in shaping the earlier ones with some subtle differences.

- When you reach bar 82, an immediately slower tempo is essential, but that must be strictly maintained to the final note.

- The composer's insistent legato reminder should deter you from any inappropriate angularity.

- Security of intonation is, of course, essential during the frequent tonal shifts – and not least as you carefully practise the intricate harmonies in bars 45–48.

5. Howells: Like as the hart desireth the waterbrooks   *Page 30*

- The mood of longing is developed with some intensity throughout this very lyrical, almost passionate anthem. The soaring phrases require excellent breathing control to help achieve their intended expressive contours.

- The detail of the dynamics should always be conveyed, and the intensity of mood developed very fully, especially at the *Where...?* climax in bars 41–47. There are articulation details (e.g., at *God*) to help the alert singer achieve the desired result.

- Notice the way the tempo indications suggest some small, but significant, increases of pace (*accelerando*) at certain places, and decreases (*rallentando*) at others, which might greatly enhance the music's emotional appeal.

- At bar 85, with the direction *dolce e ardente*, (sweetly and ardently), the dynamic level is more restrained than you might have anticipated. Aim, even so, for some tonal intensity here.

- The accompaniment is highly independent of the voices in many places, so singers need to be confident; not just of their notes, but also in habitual security of intonation.

- Altos and contraltos singing this piece for the award are expected to perform the soprano line at the places where the alto line is tacet. In bars 67–69, the original manuscript (dated 1941) shows Howells' first working of the soprano entry (revised before publication in 1943). Alto singers should perform the ossia.

6. Loosemore: O Lord, increase our faith   *Page 39*

- This is a delicately crafted, yet heartfelt, prayer in music. The dynamics should be interpreted with constant alertness, though not over a huge range. The ending can benefit from some lovely soft singing. An even tone must be evident throughout.

- The intended rhythmic energy, as you sing *In all our adversities...* might well be accompanied by a little increase in dynamics, yet nothing approaching a full-blooded *f*.

- The words must be expressed very clearly, and shaped sensitively. This will require confident breathing control, especially in the longer early phrase *Strengthen... true faith*. The final petition, *Sweet Jesus, say Amen*, ought to be sung each time as one phrase, though shaped to acknowledge the effect of its midway comma.

- An ideally chosen tempo will help produce an unrushed, but vibrantly expressive performance in miniature, full of interest for the listener.

7. Mathias: *Lift up your heads*   *Page 43*

- A most appealing anthem suitable for any of the occasions that celebrate the Kingship of Christ. Sing it with energy and confidence, but also with assured musical control!

- The composer has been careful to craft the dynamics for maximum effect. Even at the loudest moments, your tone should be bright and focused, with no hint of heaviness. Bass singers, especially, be alert to the subtle differences, so that every one of your entries makes real impact.

- Crisp articulation and rhythmic strictness will reap rewards. Be alert to the markings in the music. The text requires really focused projection. There will be a thrilling liveliness at the words *The Lord strong and mighty*, if they are sung with precision.

- Accuracy is again needed in the two quieter episodes, where there are deliberate differences to be noticed in each voice.

8. Mendelssohn: *How lovely are the messengers*   *Page 50*

- This lyrical anthem is suitable for several seasons, including Advent.

- You will be able to sing it with sensitivity and delicacy, provided the technical challenges have first been met. Amongst these, breathing, intonation and vocal blend are vital. The overall contours of the piece must also be conveyed – its calm, prayerful opening, and reprise, and the vigorous episodes at the words *to all the nations*.

- Sometimes, including specifically at the opening statements, the phrasing of the words should be unbroken, for smooth musical effect: altos and basses singing *How lovely are the messengers that preach us the gospel of peace,* all voices in bars 20-23, *To all the nations is gone forth the sound of their words,* and again at bar 38, *preach us the gospel of peace*. However, this is not a policy to be rigorously pursued – bar 25 is an example where a controlled breath can add to the impact of the phrasing. It is important that you plan your performance carefully before your exam, not trusting to luck!

- Aim to discover the optimum tempo: project a sense of the lyrical flow without undue haste, but allow the musical energy and your enjoyment to be really effectively conveyed throughout the piece.

9. Morley: Nolo mortem peccatoris
Page 60

- This Passiontide motet requires considerable sensitivity to the text, and careful musical shaping. The edition contains suggested dynamics in the keyboard reduction.

- Tonal control should be evenly matched across the vocal range, and accentuation should always be suited to the precise text, not to the bar lines you see in your copy. In choir performance, listening to all the other voices is essential. In your exam, these will be played on the piano, but your singing can still make it evident that you understand, alertly, the relative importance of your musical line at each point.

- Breathing points are clearly suggested in the text, and extra ones, which would tend to disturb the flow, should be avoided.

10. Reger: Unser lieben Frauen Traum
Page 66

- A sweet and engaging carol, suitable for Feasts of BVM.

- After a tender, restrained start, there are opportunities for rich tonal contours to be built, as the texture of voices becomes fuller towards the end.

- In whichever language you choose to sing, the clarity of your diction is vital, to enable the message of the Virgin Mary's dream to be fully appreciated.

- The third stanza (bar 33 onwards) should be strong in mood, yet a certain tenderness should remain evident in your tone and shaping. The very final phrase may be sung much more quietly, with appealing warmth.

11. Shephard: Song of Mary
Page 70

- Richard Shephard's music inspires instant singer engagement, no more so than in this lively metrical setting of Magnificat. The text is by Mary Holtby.

- Choose a tempo that helps exhibit the music's energetic and lyrical qualities but does not sound frenetic.

- There is plenty of dynamic interest and detail to be exploited. Although the final verse and refrain are marked *ff*, throughout, the quality of your tone must be dignified and unforced.

- All consonants must be clear, but the placing of end consonants should be habitually precise.

- The sung word *Magnificat* may be more pleasing to the ear with Latin, rather than Anglican, vowel sounds!

- In the exam, all voices should be ready to sing verses 1, 4 and 5, together with one other verse, and their refrains, unless the examiner requests a shorter portion of the piece. If you are singing tenor or bass, omit v.2 and the refrain; your accompanist should 'cut' from the end of bar 27 to bar 50. If you are singing an upper voice part, you should omit v.3 and its refrain, with a 'cut' from the end of bar 49 to bar 72. If you sing alto or contralto, and top Eb is difficult for you to reach, you should not choose this piece to perform.

12. Tallis: O Lord, give thy Holy Spirit   Page 79

- A prayer for the coming of the Holy Spirit, requiring delicacy and tonal balance in performance for the text to be fully appreciated by the listener.

- Intonation must be fully secure. Each voice plays some part in the gentle interplay of G and G♯, F and F♯ and C and C♯: the 'false relations' that give this music much of its individual character – provided the notes you sing are precisely the ones intended.

- A smooth performance will avoid frequent interruptions for breaths, but there is only the occasional long phrase – the beginning of the motet being one of them. If you can sing right through 5 bars, to the word *hearts*, in one well-chosen breath and with evenly shaped tone, it will have splendid initial impact.

- Dynamics are left to your discretion, but must be included, with some restraint. The words *that we may know thee* might be taken as a signal to begin some dynamic growth, climaxing at *whom thou hast sent*, followed by a quieter reprise, but this is certainly not the only suitable configuration. The sense and impact of the words must be your guide.

13. Victoria: Jesu, dulcis memoria   Page 86

Translation: Jesu, sweet remembrance, granting the heart true joys: but above honey and all things is his sweet presence.

- This motet offers the singer some warm, expressive music to perform. It requires careful precision of tuning and great sensitivity in text and phrasing.

- Beware over-frequent breathing, which would undermine the smoothness. One breath every 3 or 4 bars, as determined by the sense of the words, must be your aim.

- There are no printed dynamics, but singers must be alert to their varied use.

- Basses may sing a repeated E in mid-range in bar 11, if the low E is too challenging.

14. S. S. Wesley: O Lord my God *Page 89*

- A deceptively simple miniature in appearance, this music actually requires considerable tonal security, and some confidence in communication, to be persuasive.

- Do not attempt it very much faster than the recommended tempo, which should give you plenty of space to develop a full expressive range, provided your breathing control is really secure.

- You should also invest in the careful shaping of the words, and subtlety of accentuation, to add a warmth of expressive interest throughout the anthem. Examples: *hear, respect, forgive.*

- Take care to count each of the semibreves precisely from bar 37 onwards, and ensure they do not sound static.

- There is a choice of ending – so whichever one best suits your own voice may be used.

15. Wicks: We three kings *Page 94*

- This modern, exciting setting of the well-known Epiphany hymn calls for a very confident, exultant performance, with some brilliance of tone at the climactic moments.

- The music's energy will best be transmitted with tightly controlled rhythmic patterns, performed with a swing, at a brisk, but not frenetic, tempo. The text must always be articulated very crisply.

- The changes of tonality and chords add good interest: as an example, make sure the A♭ in bar 15 is really centred in pitch!

- Verses 1 and 3 begin with a *f* marking – not so at the start of v.2, where perhaps a phrase or two sung *mf* might offer welcome variety. Later, in v.4, there is an opportunity for more contrast, and the following refrain (if carefully rehearsed) should be built with gusto, alert to the growing pace as well as dynamics.

- Sopranos will enjoy the carefully crafted descant approaching the end of this piece. All singers must aim for a joyful and brilliant ending, with no hint of relaxation of tempo.

SYLLABUS FOR THE RSCM SILVER AWARD

The Silver award is part of the RSCM's provision for singer training which includes the *Voice for Life* training scheme, Bronze, Silver and Gold awards, and anthologies of choral music for use at all levels. The *Voice for Life* scheme enables singers to develop their musical skills and understanding within the context of their choir. The awards schemes provide opportunities for that development to be affirmed beyond the singer's own church, through the RSCM's national and international network.

The Silver Award, in some Areas named 'Bishop's Award', is open to choristers of all ages and denominations, and the syllabus has been carefully compiled with this in mind. The Silver Award is intended to recognise, by external assessment, your completion of Red level in the RSCM *Voice for Life* scheme. If successful, you will receive a certificate and may purchase the prestigious medal to wear with purple ribbon.

To begin, as well as carefully studying this syllabus, you must consult the regulations & marking criteria, the Music & Liturgy Lists and the entry form. These files are downloadable from the RSCM website, www.rscm.com, or may be requested as paper copies, from your local Area or from the RSCM Exams desk, examsdesk@rscm.com, +44 (0)1722 424843. Also check the details in your local contact information sheet.

Pre-requisites for entering RSCM awards are specified in the regulations. The exam will test four of the five modules you should have completed at *Voice for Life* Red level. They are called 'sections' in the exam.

EXAM STRUCTURE

Your exam must begin with:

- **Section A: Using the voice well** (while your accompanist is in the room with you)
- **Section B: Musical skills and understanding** (accompanied by the examiner)
- **Section C: Repertoire**
- **Section E: Choir in context**

Your exam will always start with Section A and end with Section E. Unless you state a different preference, before the exam begins, the examiner will expect to hear you sing items **A1** and **A2** in syllabus order. You will then be asked for your preferred order for singing **A3** and **A4**. (The examiner may choose to hear substantial portions, rather than complete performances, of these pieces).

Bring to the exam copies (for the examiner's use, *see reg. 10.1*) of all your Section A pieces, the contrasting piece you will be talking about in Section C2, and the different item you have chosen to mention in Section E2b). Bring any written material permitted, correctly formatted, if you wish to refer to it during the exam (*reg. 14.6*). You are also welcome to bring a water bottle.

MARK SCHEME

The maximum item mark is shown (and, in brackets, the pass mark for that item). It is not necessary to obtain a pass mark in every single item in order to pass the whole exam, but you are advised to prepare all the sections carefully, as any considerable weakness in one or more of them might affect the overall outcome. Examiners are instructed to deduct marks if incorrect items are presented or syllabus rubrics ignored. (Should this be necessary, a short explanatory comment will appear on your marksheet).

A1	A2	A3	A4	B1	B2	B3	C1+2	E
10 (6)	15 (9)	15 (9)	15 (9)	10 (6)	5 (3)	5 (3)	10 (6)	15 (9)
55%				20%			10%	15%

Section D, Belonging to the choir, is satisfied by way of the preliminary reference and testimonial that are presented with your entry. If these are not satisfactory, you will be asked to undertake more preparation and defer your exam to a later session. Although there are no specific 'Section D questions' in the exam, the final part of Section E might present you with the opportunity to mention your particular contribution to the choir.

Your exam will last about 40 minutes, the time spent on each section closely related to its mark weighting.

The **pass mark** is 60, with a **commended** result for 75 or more, and **highly commended** for 85 or more.

ENTERING FOR THE EXAM

The local **contact information sheet** provides you with forthcoming **exam dates**, **entry deadlines** and **fees**, and contact details for your **local exam administrator**.

Applicants register at <u>www.rscmawards.com</u> and compile the entry a bit at a time. You may revise it as you go. Submit it when ready. Pay electronically (if available) or by cheque. Alternatively, the entry (completed on paper) and cheque may be posted to your Area administrator.

SECTION A: USING THE VOICE WELL

You must prepare four pieces for the examiner to hear.

A1. Hymn Singing
    Maximum 10 marks (6 to pass)

Choose **three** verses to sing of a hymn, which is written in verses each of 6–8 lines (or up to 10 lines, if a refrain is included before or after each verse). The second verse should be sung unaccompanied.

You may sing the melody, **or** your own voice part for any or all of the verses if the hymn tune is written for singing in harmony.

Tell the examiner your choice, for each verse, before you begin.
See The Silver Award Music List E (available from www.rscm.com) for advice and an indicative list of choices.

The final verse may be sung, if you wish, to any descant or arrangement printed in your music (and in the copy given to the examiner), but please mention this before you begin. No extra credit will be given in the marking of this item.

A2. Psalm Singing
    Maximum 15 marks (9 to pass)

Sing
either a) **chanted psalmody,** sung to Anglican chant or to a plainsong tone.
         Sing **eight or nine consecutive verses** of a psalm, finishing with the
         Gloria, to music (chant or plainsong tone) or your own choice.
         At least two consecutive verses must be sung unaccompanied.
         Tell the examiner which verses will be sung unaccompanied, before you
         begin. (If you are singing Anglican chant, tell the examiner which voice part
         you are going to sing, and if there are nine verses, which one will be sung to
         'Second Part'). If you have attempted the Bronze Award within the past
         three years and you chose chanted psalmody to sing then, you must not
         choose the same psalm, or music, to sing again.

or b)   the whole of a **responsorial psalm** of your choice (or a substantial portion
         of it, as requested by the examiner).
         Sing the melody line. You should sing two verses, and the refrain between
         them, unaccompanied. Tell the examiner which portion will be sung
         unaccompanied, before you begin. If you have attempted the Bronze Award
         within the past three years and you chose a responsorial psalm to sing then,
         you must not choose the same psalm, or music, to sing again.

See the RSCM Silver Award Music List F for further advice.
    *The marks awarded for your psalm singing will take account of accuracy of
    chanting, but will also give significant weight to the clarity, evenness of articulation
    and sensitivity of interpretation of the text, as indicated in the marking criteria.*

A3. Anthem
   Maximum 15 marks (9 to pass)

Sing an anthem selected from **List G**. (The examiner may choose a substantial portion to hear). Sing the voice part best suited to you. Tell the examiner which part you will be singing, before you begin.

This item must be sung in the key of the music in the edition you are using, **not** transposed.

All the pieces in **List G** can be found in the *RSCM Silver Collection Books One* and *Two*.

A4. Setting or song (or second anthem)
   Maximum 15 marks (9 to pass)

Sing
either a) a setting (through-composed) of the **Magnificat**, chosen from those
         indicated in **List H**.
         Sing the voice part best suited to you. Prepare the full movement, including
         the *Gloria*. (The examiner may choose to hear the whole, or two substantial
         portions, of the piece).

or b)   a solo song, suitable for use in worship, selected from **List K**. (The examiner
         may choose a substantial portion to hear). The chosen item may be sung at
         treble or bass pitch.

or c)   **only if** the A3 anthem is selected from those in the *RSCM Silver Collection
         Book One*, a second anthem in **List G** chosen from this book. (The examiner
         may choose a substantial portion to hear). Sing the voice part best suited to
         you.

         This item must be sung in the key of the music in the edition you are using,
         not transposed.

*Marks awarded in Section A will take account of accuracy and musical
intention in your performances, with equal weight given to evidence of your
vocal technique. Refer to the marking criteria for more details.*

SECTION B: MUSICAL SKILLS AND UNDERSTANDING

B1. *Singing at first & second sight*
   Maximum 10 marks (6 to pass)

The examiner will ask you to sing, with the given English text, a short piece of two or three phrases. The outline accompaniment shown will be played by the examiner. It will be in one of these keys: D, E♭, F, A♭, B♭ major *or* C, D, F, G, B minor, and it will be pitched in the range low C – upper D. You may use either treble (G) or bass (F) stave. You will be asked to read aloud the given words on the page, to help familiarise yourself with them.

The key chord and your first note will be named and sounded, and repeated after 15 seconds' preparation time. Set your own tempo (there will be no introduction) and sing the piece with careful attention to the printed dynamics, as well as musical phrasing and articulation.

A second attempt will be offered (unless your first try was faultless, including all the expressive detail, and gaining the maximum mark). Before it, **the examiner will offer you a moment's help** with one significant point of error (such as a miscounted rhythm, mispitched interval or overlooked dynamic marking). The key chord and your first note will then be given again. Credit will be given for improvement at your second attempt.

The melody will be in 2/4, 3/4, 4/4, 2/2 or 6/8 time, not necessarily beginning on the first beat of the bar, and it may include rests, ties and dotted notes. One non-diatonic note may be encountered, with intervals of up to and including a 6th, and a perfect octave. A range of dynamic variations between *p* and *f* including a 'hairpin' may be indicated.

A suitable Italian performance direction will head the piece, and a change of tempo might be indicated near the end. The outline accompaniment will double the melody briefly in some places; often, it will be more independent.

B2. *Aural exercises*
   Maximum 5 marks (3 to pass)

Candidates will be expected to:

   a) Clap or tap, in strict time, the **pulse** of a melody in simple or compound time, not necessarily beginning on the first beat of the bar, during its **second** playing by the examiner. Then you should state that the melody was in 2 time, 3 time or 4 time.

   b) Sing, as echoes, two 2-bar phrases, each played to you twice in your vocal range. They will begin on the first beat of the bar, in 3/4, 4/4 or 6/8 time. You should repeat each phrase musically, and in strict time, immediately after its **second** playing. To begin, the key chord and first note of the opening phrase will be sounded, and two bars of pulse will be counted aloud by the examiner as introduction to the initial playing of the opening phrase. You may use any vowel sound or sol-fa in sung exercises.

c) Sing the middle or lowest note, as requested by the examiner, of a tonic triad, after you have heard it twice, and say whether the triad was major or minor.
(The key note will be sounded, and the triad, in close position in any inversion, played in your vocal range). Two or three examples will be given.

d) Sing some requested intervals, selected from major 2nd, major or minor 3rd or 6th, and perfect 4th or 5th. You will be asked to sing a given key note, in the lower range of your voice, before the examiner tells you the interval you should sing above it. Two or three examples, on different key notes, will be given.

In c) you may be offered a second chance if you initially choose an incorrect note of the triad to sing. However, this will be reflected in the overall assessment, as indicated in the marking criteria.

B3. Technical questions
   Maximum 5 marks (3 to pass)

The examiner will choose **either** your **A3** *Anthem*, **or** your **A4** *Setting or song (or second anthem)* piece, and will refer you back to your copy of it, as a starting point for questions to test your familiarity with:

- Notes of both the treble (G) and bass (F) staves, which may include some on leger lines
- Time values of notes, including dotted and syncopated patterns
- Time signatures (simple and compound times)
- Key signatures (of major and minor keys, and their relationships, up to five sharps and five flats)
- Dynamic markings
- Performance instructions, as learned at *Voice for Life* **Red** level (p.28 in the Singer's Workbook), but also including any of the Italian words you have already encountered at earlier levels.

You may be given the opportunity to correct an answer if you make a mistake. However, this will be reflected in the overall assessment, as indicated in the marking criteria.
No extra written material is permitted in this section of the exam.

SECTION C: REPERTOIRE
Maximum 10 marks (6 to pass)

C1. *Understanding of your chosen anthem*

You will be asked **two** questions about the **A3** *Anthem* you sang earlier in the exam. One question will concern **each** of the following topics:

its **text and music** (origins; style; mood, contrasts and meaning; how the music reflects the text)

its **context** (historical, including the musical period; liturgical appropriateness in your Sunday service; music written by different composers in this musical period, or in other periods in the same genre).

Your knowledge should build on, and show progression beyond, the level of studies required at *Bronze Award*. Helpful advice is found in **Module C,** *Voice for Life* **Red** level (p.30–32 in the Singer's Workbook).

In addition to the typical questions indicated at Bronze standard, the examiner might ask you questions such as:

(text & music) "Summarise in your own words the meaning of this text."

"Give an example where the music of your anthem varies to reflect the meaning of the text."

(context) "In which musical period did this composer live?"

"Would this anthem be suitable for a particular Festival service in the year, and can you say why?"

"Name a piece written about the same time by a different composer, and tell me if it is similar."

Either of the questions may lead on to a short discussion in which your background musical and liturgical knowledge might be explored a little more.

2. Understanding of a contrasted anthem

Give a short statement* about a contrasted anthem you have chosen from the *RSCM Silver Collection Book One*, following the **Hints and tips** on p.30 of your Red Singer's Workbook. Remember to say how this anthem contrasts with the one you sang in item **A3**. If you wish, you may bring your Workbook with you, having written your statement on p.32, and read it aloud.

The examiner will then ask you **one** straightforward question about the anthem, its music or its background. *Please be ready, if requested, to show the examiner your copy of the chosen piece before beginning your short statement.*

> ** Statements should be not more than half a minute long. You are welcome to read this statement straight from your Red Singer's Workbook or from one sheet of paper (headed C2). Bring a copy of this book or sheet with you, for the examiner's use.*

All singers on the Voice for Life *scheme are expected to develop their knowledge and understanding of the repertoire.* **The Voice for Life Guide to Musicianship** *(order no: F0120) and* **Using Voice for Life** *(order no: F0121) provide helpful training material for this section of the examination.*

SECTION D: BELONGING TO THE CHOIR

This module is satisfied by way of the preliminary reference and testimonial that are presented with your entry. These give the opportunity for your special contributions to the life of your church or chapel, and your role in the choir or singing group, to be recognised. Your attendance rate (singing at rehearsals and services) must be certified, and over the past 6 months is expected to have been at least "satisfactory" (75%) if not "impeccable" (95%), after allowing for any excused absence (as determined locally).

Before entering for the Silver Award, as part of your commitment to your choir or singing group, you should have taken part in at least one special day of music making, within the previous two years (and since taking your Bronze Award, if you have done so). This might have been attending your RSCM Area Festival, a singing course, workshop or other event (organised by your RSCM Area, or nationally), or (at the discretion of your local exam administrator) a special music course or visit organised by your own choir or a musical event with a school or other local organisation. Your attendance at this event, with the date, should be certified in the reference.

SECTION E: CHOIR IN CONTEXT
Maximum 15 marks (9 to pass)

E1. *Bible*

Origin and meaning of biblical texts
Study the following six liturgical texts, familiar in all Christian traditions. The examiner will choose **one** of them, to assess your knowledge of the words and meaning. You should also be prepared to discuss its biblical origins
   Our Father; Holy Holy Holy; Glory to God; Lamb of God; Magnificat; Nunc Dimittis.

E2. *Liturgy*

a) Understanding of Communion service, Mass or Eucharist
Describe in some detail the form of service you have attended, **from the Thanksgiving (Eucharistic) Prayer, up to and including taking communion.** Mention the sung items (if any) in this part of the service.
Be ready to discuss your understanding of the service as a whole, as well as the part of it you have studied in more detail. You may bring a service book or card and, having first shown it to the examiner, you may then refer to it very briefly during your answers.

b) Epiphany to Pentecost
Give a short statement* detailing **three** holy days that might be celebrated in your church or school between (but **not** including) the Feasts of Epiphany and Pentecost. Mention them in chronological order, relating each of them to the main Christian seasons of Lent, Passiontide and Easter.
Not more than one of the weekdays in Holy Week may be chosen, and do not choose Easter Day (as this featured in the Bronze Award).

Please refer to List L for more guidance.
Select **one** of the three holy days, *or* **a service of initiation** in your own liturgical tradition (baptism, confirmation, reception into church membership) which might happen in your church or school during or around this period. Declare it on your entry form as your **Section E chosen service.**

Declare on your entry form **an anthem or song** suitable for this service, different from your other choices for this exam, and bring a copy of it (for the examiner's use) with you.
You must also prepare, and bring with you, **a suitable Bible reading** for your chosen service.

The examiner will ask you to read out loud a short portion, no more than three verses, from your Bible reading, and will then ask you some questions:

to explore your understanding of the Bible reading in the context of the chosen service

about your detailed knowledge of the musical item you chose and its suitability for the service; this may include explaining the meaning (and relevance to your choice) of any of the words in the text.

Please be ready, if requested, to show the examiner the copy of your piece, and the Bible reading, before the questions are asked.

c) One other holy day mentioned in your statement

The examiner will choose another of the holy days you mentioned in your short statement. You will be asked a straightforward question about its meaning and significance. Be ready to suggest, with good reason, any suitable piece of music which might be sung (by a singing group, choir or congregation) during a service on that holy day.

E3. Ministry

Music, Prayer & Worship

Give a short statement* **explaining**, with reference to one of the 6 pieces of music you have already produced in this exam (whether in Section A, or C2, or item 2b), above), **how music helps people to pray.**

You should comment on how both the music and the words of this piece may be helpful in worship.

The examiner may then ask you questions to explore your understanding of musical ministry in more detail, and to encourage you to show, if not already evident, your awareness of the contribution the choir or singing group might make to the worshipping life of your church or chapel.

> *Please be ready, if requested, to show the examiner your copy of the chosen piece before beginning your short statement.*

> ** Statements should be not more than half a minute long. You will not be asked to perform any examples in Section E, but you may refer very briefly to your copies of music and a service book. Your understanding of issues raised in this section, which could affect the overall mark, might vary according to your age and experience. Your answers should be expressed in straightforward language. Although you are allowed to read statements from written notes (if correctly formatted), this might be reflected in the assessment of the item, as indicated in the marking criteria.*

RSCM SILVER AWARD MARKING CRITERIA

SECTION A: USING THE VOICE WELL

These two areas are to be weighted 50/50 throughout Section A performances:

Accuracy & musical intention	*Technique*
VERY GOOD **A1 Hymn: (10); A2–A4: (14–15)**	
• Text clearly, evenly, sympathetically sung • Mood communicated vividly • Assured sense of style	• Impeccable tonal confidence and control • Assured use of dynamic opportunities • Breathing meticulously planned and executed
GOOD **A1 Hymn: (8–9); A2–A4: (12–13)**	
• Confident, engaging performance • Persuasive phrasing, and quite sensitive vocal articulation • Secure posture and effective communication	• Consistently reliable intonation, including precision in unaccompanied passages • Clear diction • Mainly secure breathing technique • Some effective dynamic interest
SATISFACTORY BUT SOME TECHNICAL LAPSES **A1 Hymn: (7); A2–A4: (10–11)**	
• Mainly secure, despite small lapses in tonal control, breathing or diction • One error in notes or pulse, with prompt recovery • Consistent sense of style and phrasing	• Intonation mostly secure, with infrequent lapses and/or a little drift in pitch when singing unaccompanied • Consistent tonal projection, if a little weaker at extremes of range
A1 Hymn: (6); A2–A4: (9)	
• Cautious connection with the meaning • Style and phrasing tentatively developed	• Accurate, but without much dynamic interest • Text audible, but not always very clear
MORE SIGNIFICANT TECHNICAL CONCERN **A1 Hymn: (5); A2–A4: (7–8)**	
• Lack of confidence or security at times • Insufficient connection with the meaning	• Lack of technical consistency • Noticeably weak breathing control
A1 Hymn: (3–4); A2–A4: (5–6)	
• Loss of security, with poor recovery • Lack of sensitivity in phrasing • Poor posture and communication	• A severe technical problem marring the quality of sound • Intonation a frequent anxiety
MUCH MORE PREPARATION NEEDED **A1 Hymn: (2); A2–A4: (3–4)**	
• Lack of any musical shape or expression • Major breakdown in continuity • Incomplete performance	• More than one severe technical difficulty (tone/diction/breathing/intonation) • Extreme lack of confidence
THIS ITEM WAS NOT ATTEMPTED (0)	

SECTION A2	SECTION B: MUSICAL SKILLS AND UNDERSTANDING
Chanted psalmody	B1 : Singing at first & second sight
VERY GOOD	
A2: (14–15)	B1: (10)
• Faultless pointing • Very clear, expressive text • Sensitive phrasing/shaping	• Faultless first attempt, including convincing expressive detail, and clear, sensitive treatment of text
GOOD	
A2: (12–13)	B1: (8–9)
• Confident style/pointing • Precise text & diction • Reliable intonation, including chanting notes and in unaccompanied verses	• Confident attempts, not totally accurate • Slips largely corrected at second attempt • Some expressive details noticed • Accurate text, at one attempt if not both
SATISFACTORY BUT SOME TECHNICAL LAPSES	SOME HESITATION OR MISTAKES
A2: (10–11)	B1: (6–7)
• One text/pointing error, with prompt recovery • Mainly evenly shaped text & phrases, with some sensitivity to the meaning	• Mainly keeping going • Some rhythmic security despite slips • Pitch outline evident, but significant slips • Tone and intonation generally secure • Improvement at second attempt
A2: (9)	
• Cautious approach • Tentative phrasing/shaping	
MORE SIGNIFICANT TECHNICAL CONCERN	
A2: (5–8)	B1: (3–5)
• Some text/pointing errors • Lack of momentum/shape in chanting • Text sometimes unclear • Un-musically phrased, or stilted in musical effect	• Many errors in notes and rhythms • Severe lack of technical consistency • Little or no improvement at second attempt • Significant difficulty with text or underlay
MUCH MORE PREPARATION NEEDED	
A2: (3–4)	B1: (2)
• Frequent inaccuracies in notes/text/ pointing	• Considerable breakdown in progress • Extreme lack of confidence • Incomplete attempts
THIS ITEM WAS NOT ATTEMPTED (0)	

B2: AURAL	B3: TECHNICAL
VERY GOOD	
B2: (5)	B3: (5)
• Faultless, prompt response in each item	• Comprehensive and fully accurate technical answers
GOOD	
B2: (4)	B3: (4)
• All responses reasonably secure, rhythmic and in tune • No undue delay in answers	• Alert, mainly precise answers • Able to apply technical knowledge beyond set piece • No undue delay in answers
SOME HESITATION OR MISTAKES	
B2: (3)	B3: (3)
• At least half the items accurate • Some slips corrected when prompted or at second attempt • Only one item significantly weak	• Basic accuracy, but a few slips • Some slips corrected when prompted • Only one technical aspect significantly weak • Other clef known in outline
MORE SIGNIFICANT CONCERN	
B2: (2)	B3: (2)
• Most items incorrect • Sung responses out of tune • Lack of aural awareness • Persistent tendency to guess	• Inaccuracies in most items • Lack of technical familiarity • Persistent tendency to guess • Little or no knowledge of other clef
MUCH MORE PREPARATION NEEDED	
B2: (1)	B3: (1)
• Inaccurate and hesitant response in each item • Some questions unanswered	• Inaccurate and hesitant response in each item • Some questions unanswered
THIS ITEM WAS NOT ATTEMPTED (0)	

SECTION C: REPERTOIRE	SECTION E: CHOIR IN CONTEXT
VERY GOOD	
C: (10)	E: (14–15)
• Cogent answers to each question, and musical details securely recalled • Convincing background knowledge • Alert, with no prompting, in discussion	• Very convincing, in plain language, in all five items • Cogent detail, without discursion/ excursion • No prompting or notes needed in discussion
GOOD	
C: (8–9)	E: (12–13)
• Some understanding evident in each answer • Mainly detailed responses in discussion • Well prepared and presented answers • Evidence of some background knowledge	• Some understanding evident in all five items, with mainly detailed responses in discussion • Well prepared and presented answers • Minimal use of notes to prompt the memory • E3 presented convincingly
MAINLY RESPONSIVE	
C: (6–7)	E: (10–11)
• Basic accuracy, but rather superficial or lacking in some detail • Knowledge unearthed with prompting, or several references to notes • Answers limited by simple language • C2 presented accurately, if a little briefly or hesitantly	• Mainly accurate answers, but lacking in some detail • Answers limited by simple language • Only one item significantly weak
	E: (9)
	• Superficial accuracy, but significant losses of detail • Knowledge unearthed with prompting, or several references to notes or statements • Limited understanding in more than one item
GAPS IN KNOWLEDGE & UNDERSTANDING	
C: (3–5)	E: (7–8)
• Inaccurate replies to two or more questions • Musical periods or dates very confused • Persistent tendency to guess • C2 presented unconvincingly, with lack of accurate contrasting features	• Inaccurate, incomplete or confused answers, in response to E2 service/holy days, or elsewhere • E2 Bible passage not contextually understood
	E: (5–6)
	• Inadequate answers in two or more items • E3 presented very unconvincingly
MUCH MORE PREPARATION NEEDED	
C: (2)	E: (3–4)
• Inaccurate and hesitant response throughout • Some questions unanswered	• Inaccurate and sketchy response to all questions • At least two items appeared totally unprepared • Some questions received no answer at all
THIS ITEM WAS NOT ATTEMPTED (0)	